Christmas Duets for Piano &

Table of Contents:

Arrangements by: Kathryn Carpenter
(c) 2020 Kathryn Carpenter
www.kathrynleecarpenter.com

God Rest Ye Merry, Gentlemen

Unknown, English Melody
Arranged by: Kathryn Carpenter

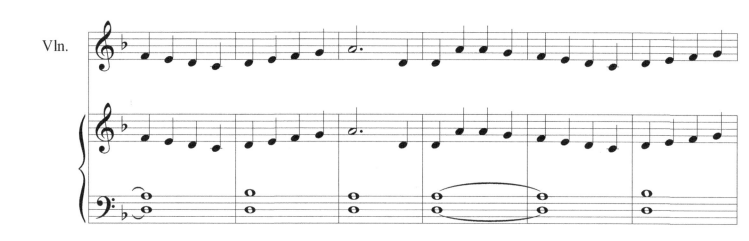

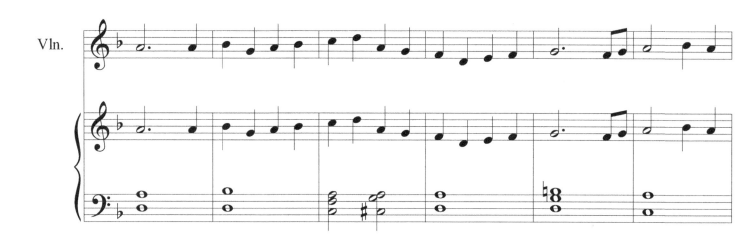

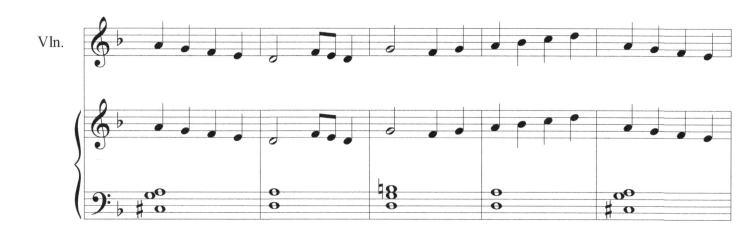

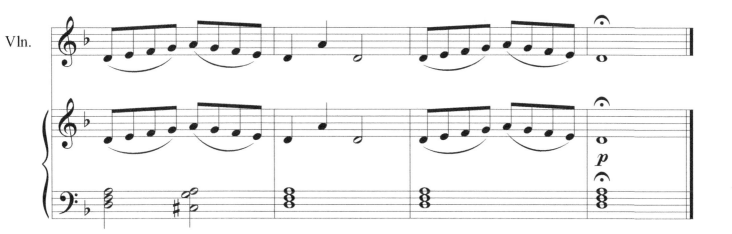

Deck the Halls

Composed by: Welsh Carol,
Thomas Oliphant
Arranged by: Kathryn Carpenter

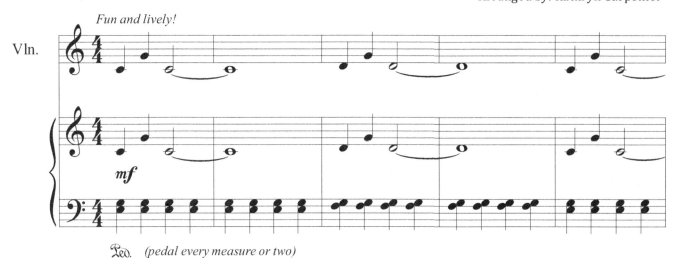

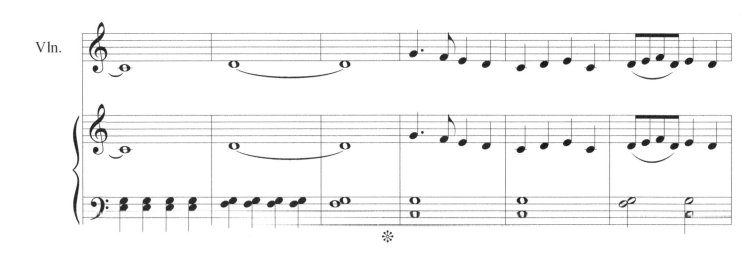

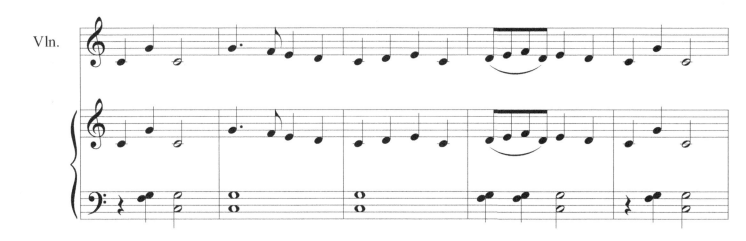

Ped. (with pedal)

8

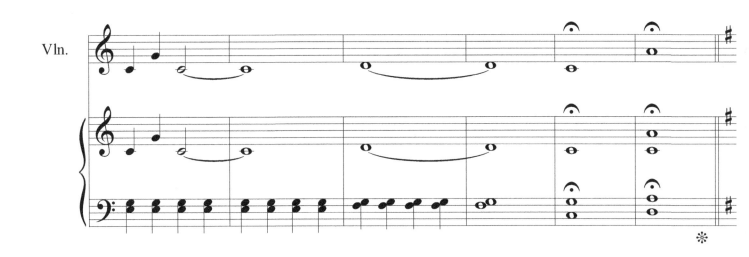

Ped. (with pedal, pedal every measure or two)

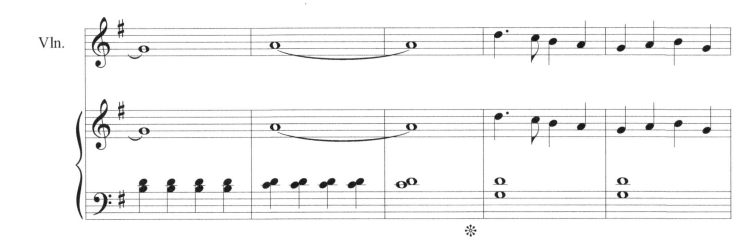

Vln.

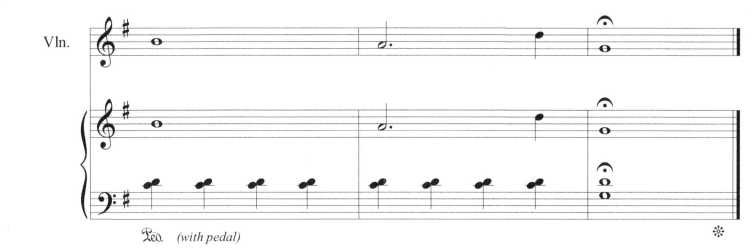

Ped. *(with pedal)*

Angels We Have Heard on High

Composed by: Chadwick, Unknown, Barnes
Arranged by: Kathryn Carpenter

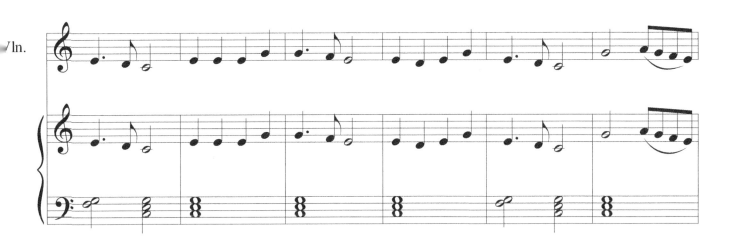

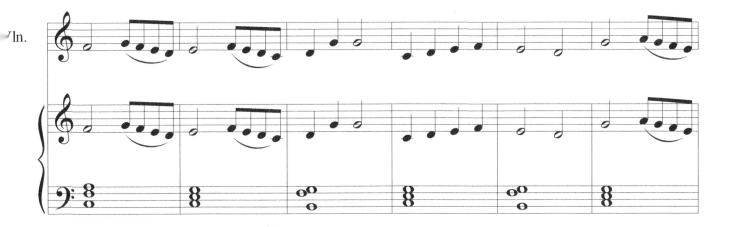

12

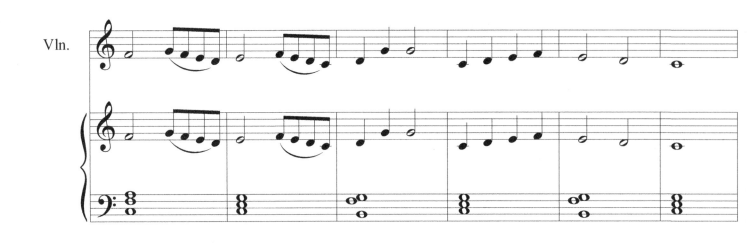

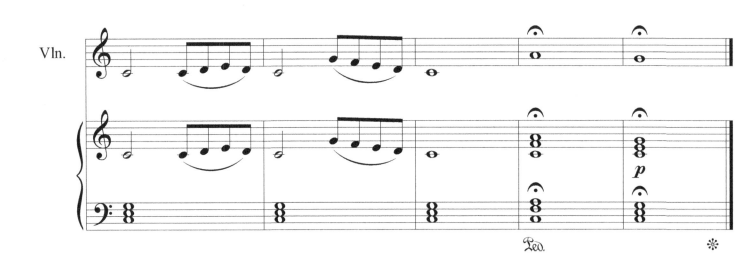

Jingle Bells

Composed by: James Lord Pierpont
Arranged by: Kathryn Carpenter

14

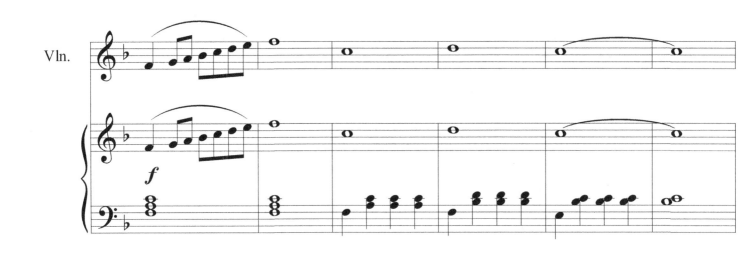

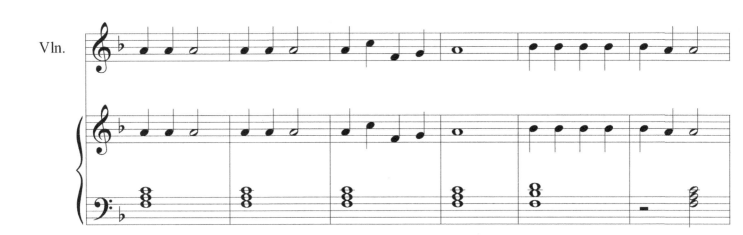

Ped. *(with pedal)* *

18

Away in a Manger

Composed by: Unknown, McFarland, Murray
Arranged by: Kathryn Carpenter

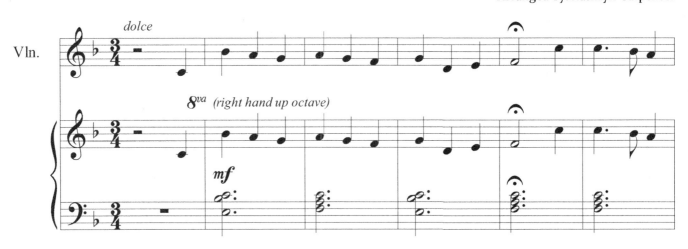

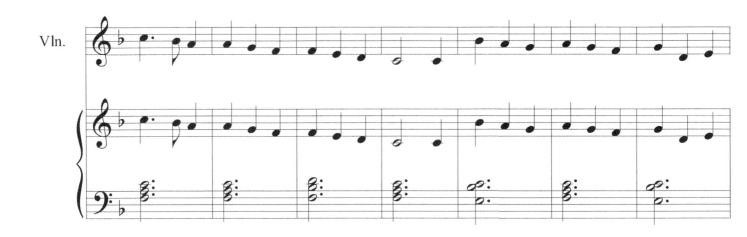

Vln.

loco

Ped. *(with pedal)*

We Wish You a Merry Christmas

English Christmas Carol
Arranged by: Kathryn Carpenter

Jolly Old St. Nicholas

Composed by: McCaskey, Murray, Hanby
Arranged by: Kathryn Carpenter

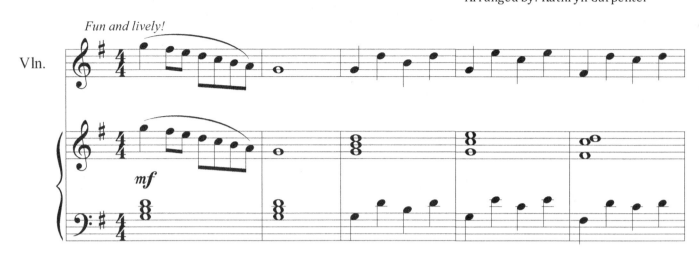

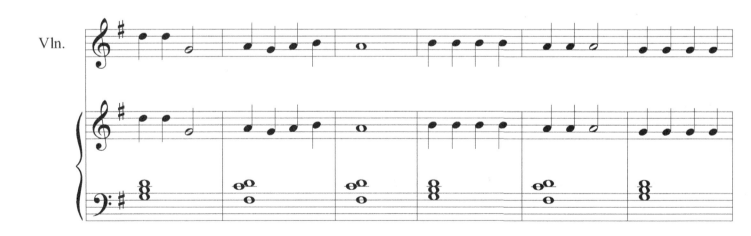

Silent Night

Composed by: Mohr, Young, Unknown, Gruber
Arranged by: Kathryn Carpenter

Vln.

Vln.

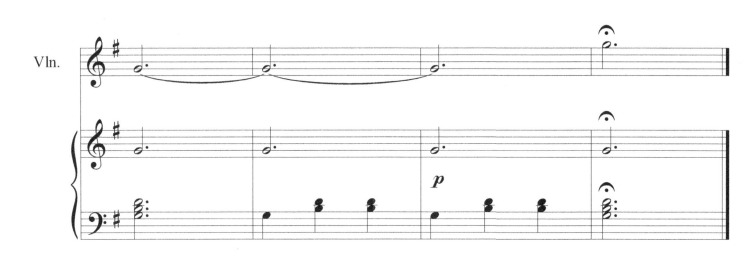

p

Up on the Housetop

Composed by: Benjamin Hanby, 1864
Arranged by: Kathryn Carpenter

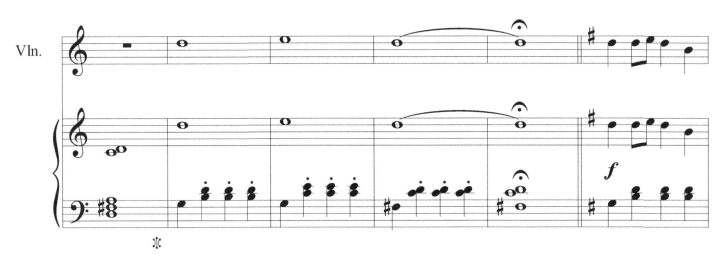

It Came Upon the Midnight Clear

Composed by: Sears, Willis
Arranged by: Kathryn Carpenter

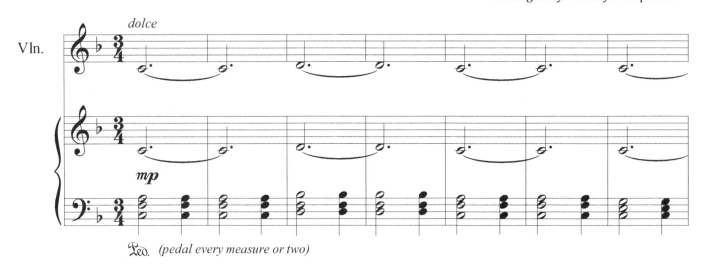

Vln.

dolce

mp

𝄆 *(pedal every measure or two)*

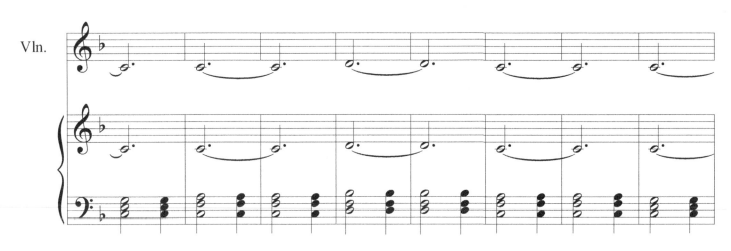

Vln.

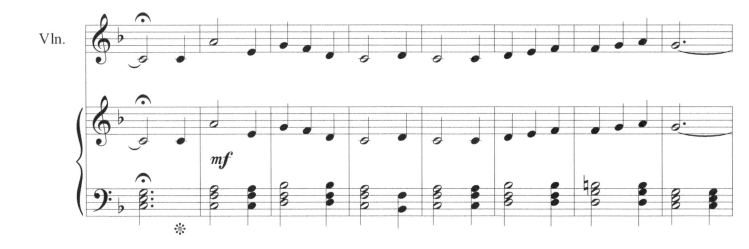

Vln.

mf

32

Here We Come a Caroling

English Christmas Carol
Arranged by: Kathryn Carpenter

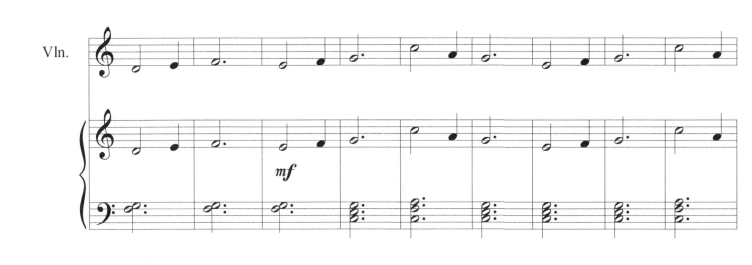

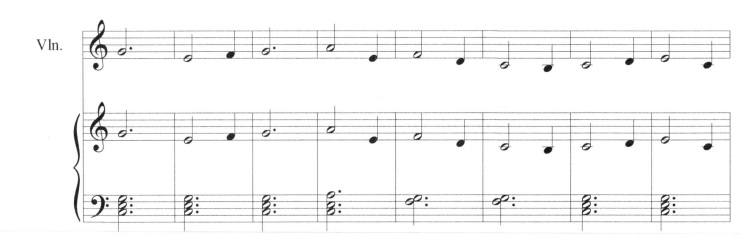

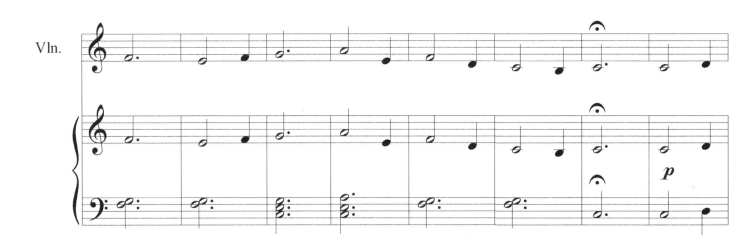

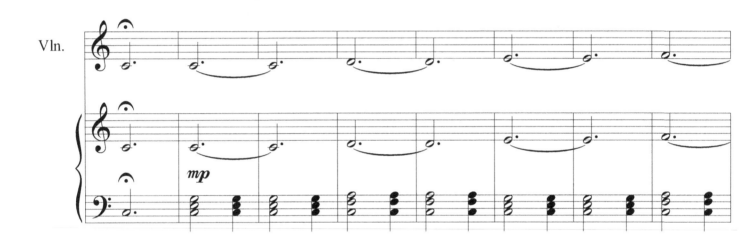

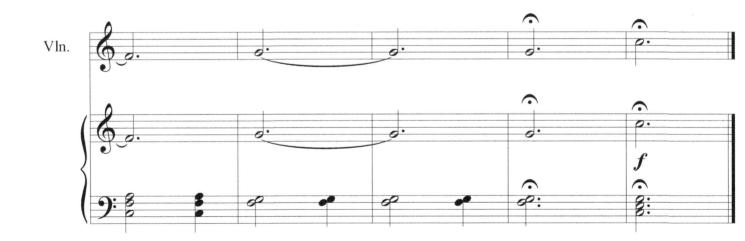

What Child is This?

Composed by: Dix, English Melody
Arranged by: Kathryn Carpenter

Ped. *(pedal every measure or two)*

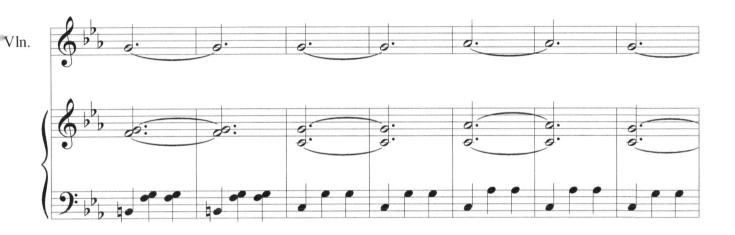

38

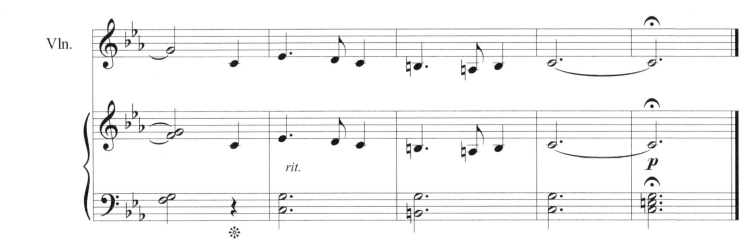

O Little Town of Bethlehem

Composed by: Brooks, Redner
Arranged by: Kathryn Carpenter

42

44

Go Tell it on the Mountain

Composed by: Unknown, African American Melody
Arranged by: Kathryn Carpenter

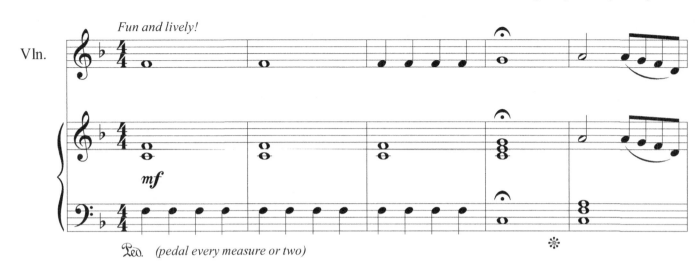

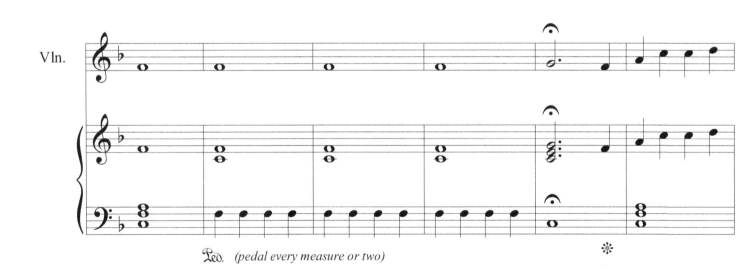

Ped. *(pedal every measure or two)*

Vln.

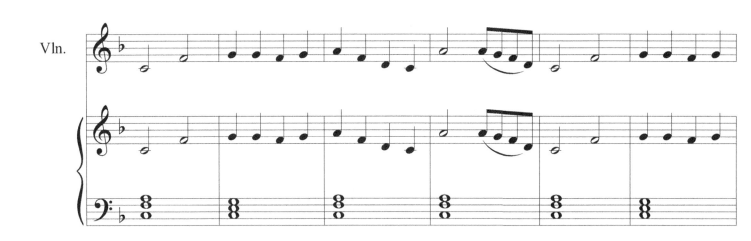

Vln.

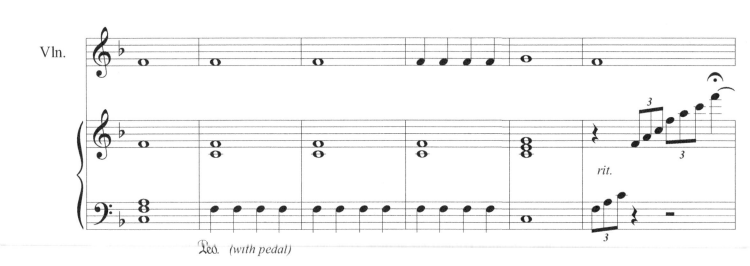

Ped. (with pedal)

Vln.

The Twelve Days of Christmas

Composed by: English Christmas Carol, Austin
Arranged by: Kathryn Carpenter

48

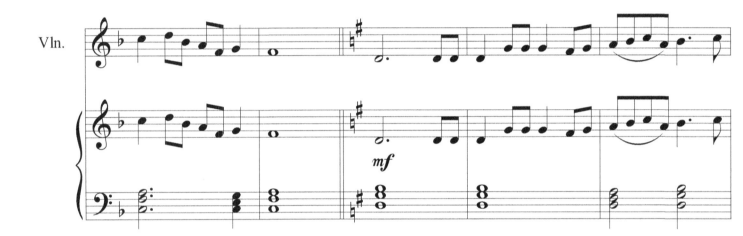

O Holy Night

Composed by: Cappeau, Dwight, Adam
Arranged by: Kathryn Carpenter

54

Made in the USA
Las Vegas, NV
23 November 2024

12397801R00031